Math Mammoth Grade 1 Skills Review Workbook Answer Key

By Maria Miller

Copyright 2017-2024 Taina Maria Miller

ISBN 978-1-942715-28-3

2017 EDITION

All rights reserved. No part of this book may be reproduced or transmitted in any form or by any means, electronic or mechanical, or by any information storage and retrieval system, without permission in writing from the author.

Copying permission: For having purchased this book, the copyright owner grants to the teacher-purchaser a limited permission to reproduce this material for use with his or her students; however, no permission is granted for commercial resale of the material. In other words, the teacher-purchaser MAY print or otherwise make copies of the pages to provide them at no cost to his or her students. The copyright holder also grants permission to the purchaser to make an electronic copy of the material for the purpose of back-up in the event of the loss or corruption of the primary copy. If you have other needs, such as licensing for a school or tutoring center, contact the author at https://www.MathMammoth.com/contact.php

Contents

	Work-text page	Answer key page
Chapter 1: Addition Within 0-10		
Skills Review 1	7	4
Skills Review 2	8	4
Skills Review 3	9	5
Skills Review 4	10	5
Skills Review 5	11	6
Skills Review 6	12	6
Skills Review 7	13	7
Skills Review 8	14	7
Skills Review 9	15	7
Skills Review 10	16	8
Skills Review 11	17	8
Skills Review 12	18	8
Chapter 2: Subtraction Within 0-10		
Skills Review 13	19	9
Skills Review 14	20	9
Skills Review 15	21	9
Skills Review 16	22	10
Skills Review 17	23	10
Skills Review 18	24	11
Skills Review 19	25	11
Skills Review 20	26	12
Skills Review 21	27	12
Skills Review 22	28	12
Chapter 3: Place Value Within 0-100		
Skills Review 23	29	13
Skills Review 24	30	13
Skills Review 25	31	13
Skills Review 26	32	13
Skills Review 27	33	14
Skills Review 28	34	14
Skills Review 29	35	14
Chapter 4: Addition and Subtraction Facts		
Skills Review 30	36	15
Skills Review 31	37	15
Skills Review 32	38	15
Skills Review 33	39	16
Skills Review 34	40	16
Skills Review 35	41	17
Skills Review 36	42	17

	Work-text page	Answer key page
Chapter 5: Time		
Skills Review 37	43	18
Skills Review 38	44	18
Skills Review 39	45	18
Skills Review 40	46	19
Skills Review 41	47	19
Chapter 6: Shapes and Measuring		
Skills Review 42	48	20
Skills Review 43	49	20
Skills Review 44	50	20
Skills Review 45	51	21
Skills Review 46	52	21
Skills Review 47	53	21
Skills Review 48	54	22
Skills Review 49	55	22
Skills Review 50	56	22
Skills Review 51	57	23
Chapter 7: Adding and Subtracting Within 1-100		
Skills Review 52	58	24
Skills Review 53	59	24
Skills Review 54	60	24
Skills Review 55	61	25
Skills Review 56	62	25
Skills Review 57	63	25
Skills Review 58	64	26
Skills Review 59	65	26
Skills Review 60	66	26
Skills Review 61	67	27
Skills Review 62	68	27
Skills Review 63	69	27
Skills Review 64	70	28
Chapter 8: Coins		
Skills Review 65	71	29
Skills Review 66	72	29
Skills Review 67	73	29
Skills Review 68	74	29
Skills Review 69	75	30
Skills Review 70	76	30

Chapter 1: Addition Within 0-10

Skills Review 1, p. 7

1. a. 6 + 2 = 8   b. 4 + 3 = 7

2.

3.
a. 3

b. 5

c. 4

d. 6

Skills Review 2, p. 8

1.
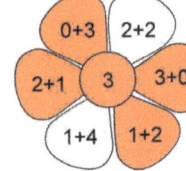 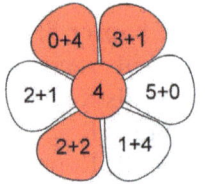

2. a. <   b. <   c. >   d. <

3. Answers will vary. Please check the student's work.

4. a. 4, 4   b. 6, 6

Skills Review 3, p. 9

1. a. 6 > 3   b. 6 > 4
2. a. 2   b. 3   c. 1
3.

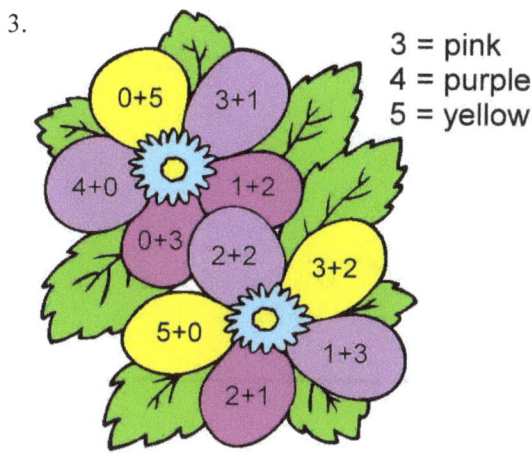

4. a. 1 + 3   b. 1 + 1   c. 5 + 0   d. 1 + 2

Skills Review 4, p. 10

1.

2.

a. 0 + 1 = 1	b. 1 + 1 = 2	c. 2 + 2 = 4
0 + 2 = 2	1 + 2 = 3	2 + 3 = 5
0 + 3 = 3	1 + 3 = 4	2 + 4 = 6
0 + 4 = 4	1 + 4 = 5	2 + 5 = 7
0 + 5 = 5	1 + 5 = 6	2 + 6 = 8

3. a. >   b. <   c. <   d. >

Skills Review 5, p. 11

1.
1 + 5 yellow	0 + 5 green	3 + 3 yellow	0 + 6 yellow
2 + 4 yellow	6 + 0 yellow	2 + 3 green	4 + 2 yellow
3 + 2 green	4 + 1 green	5 + 1 yellow	1 + 4 green

2. Please check the student's drawings.
 a. 3   b. 1 + 2   c. 3 + 3   d. 3 + 2   e. 2 + 4   f. 2 + 3

3. a. False 4 > 5   b. False 4 < 3   c. False 2 < 0

4. a. 6, 4, 5, 3   b. 5, 4, 3, 6   c. 2, 5, 5, 6

Skills Review 6, p. 12

1. Answers will vary. Please check the student's work. See example below.

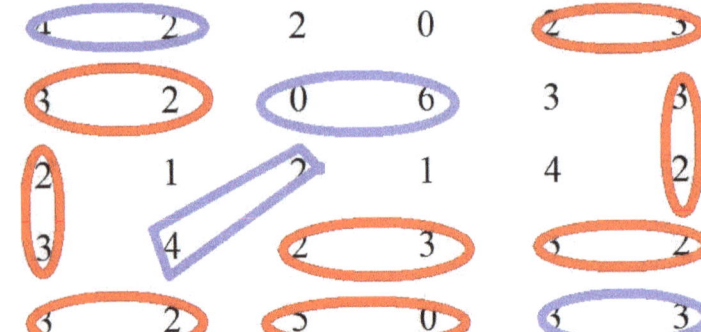

2. a.
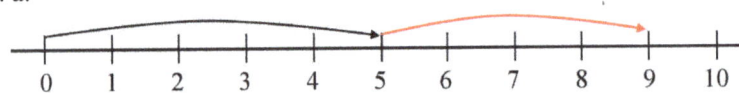

 b.
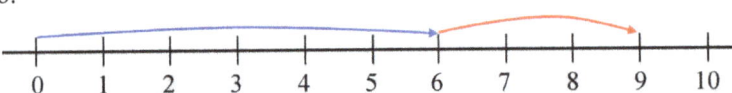

3.
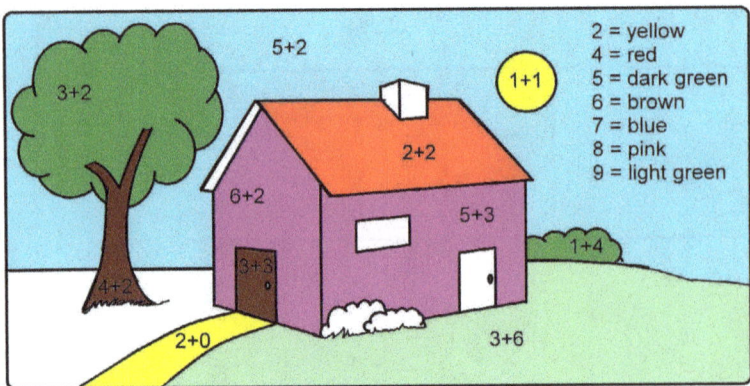

Skills Review 7, p. 13

1. orange   orange   yellow   yellow
   yellow   green   green   green
   green   yellow   green   orange

2. a.
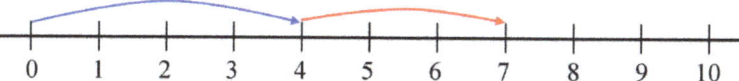

   b.
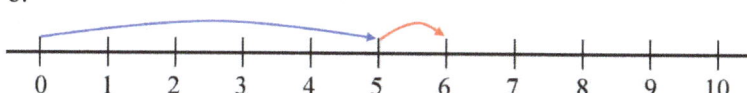

3. a. 7   b. 7   c. 7   d. 4   e. 6

4. a. Mom baked seven pies.   b. Two of the animals are not dogs.

Skills Review 8, p. 14

1. a. 8   b. 8   c. 7   d. 8   e. 6

2. a. She picked eight flowers.
   b. She needs two more buttons.

3. a. 6, 5, 4, 3   b. 6, 5, 4, 3   c. 1, 2, 3, 4

4. a. =   b. <   c. >   d. >

Skills Review 9, p. 15

1. Please check the student's work.

2. a. 9   b. 7   c. 9   d. 6   e. 9

3. a. The girls found eight pretty shells
   b. Mom made four cheese sandwiches.
   c. The children have a total of seven pets.

Skills Review 10, p. 16

1. Emma ate three cookies.

2.
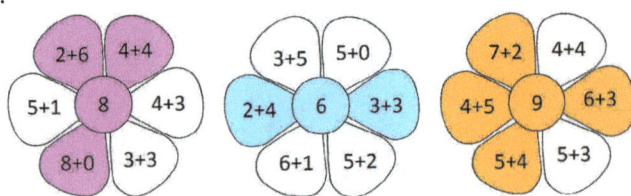

3. a.
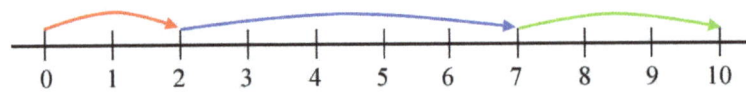

b.
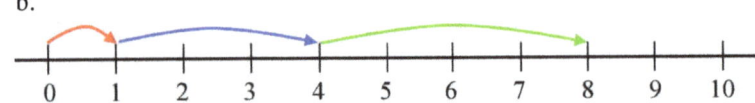

4. a. <   b. =   c. >   d. >

Skills Review 11, p. 17

1. 2 > 0   7 < 9   4 > 1
   4 < 6   5 > 2   8 < 9

2.

4	+	5	=	9
+				
3	+	2	=	5
=		+		+
7		4		3
		=		=
2	+	6	=	8

3. a. 12   b. 7   c. 9   d. 9   e. 7

Skills Review 12, p. 18

1. a. 9 < 10   b. 5 = 5   c. 8 > 7

2. a. 1, 2, 3, 4   b. 4, 5, 6, 7   c. 7, 6, 5, 4

3. a. Three pencils are missing.
   b. There are ten kittens in the basket.

Chapter 2: Subtraction Within 0-10

Skills Review 13, p. 19

1. a. 9   b. 8   c. 5   d. 9   e. 7
2. a. 6 − 4 = 2   b. 4 − 2 = 2   c. 5 − 3 = 2   d. 8 − 5 = 3   e. 9 − 2 = 7   f. 7 − 3 = 4
3. a. 6   b. 8   c. 4   d. 2   e. 5   f. 9

Skills Review 14, p. 20

1. a. 7 − 4 = <u>3</u>

   b. 6 − 2 = <u>4</u>

   c. 9 − 3 = <u>6</u>

2. Please check the student's work for the circle illustrations.
   a. 3   b. 0   c. 6   d. 2   e. 7   f. 6

3. a. 7 − 5 = 2. <u>There are two kittens left in the basket.</u>
   b. 6 + 4 = 10. <u>Eric has ten grapes.</u>

Skills Review 15, p. 21

1. a. 6 + 1 = 7   b. 4 + 3 = 7   c. 2 + 5 = 7
      7 − 1 = 6   7 − 3 = 4   7 − 5 = 2

2. a. 8 < 10   b. 4 < 5   c. 7 > 4   d. 8 = 8   e. 2 = 2   f. 6 > 5

3. Todd has nine pets.

4. a. 8 − 2 = 6   b. 5 − 2 = 3   c. 9 − 2 = 7   d. 6 − 2 = 4
      8 − 3 = 5   5 − 3 = 2   9 − 3 = 6   6 − 3 = 3

Skills Review 16, p. 22

1.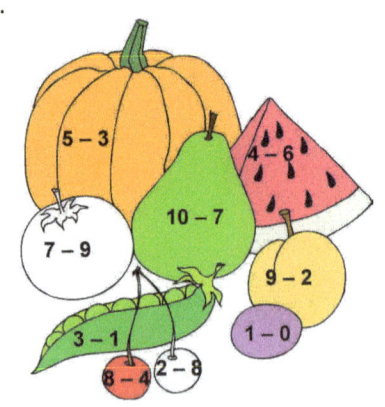

2.
7 − 0 = 7
7 − 1 = 6
7 − 2 = 5
7 − 3 = 4
7 − 4 = 3
7 − 5 = 2
7 − 6 = 1
7 − 7 = 0

3. a. 5   b. 3   c. 0   d. 5   e. 5

4.
a. 5 + 4 = 9
   9 − 4 = 5

b. 8 + 2 = 10
   10 − 2 = 8

Skills Review 17, p. 23

1. a. 8 − 3 = 5

   b. 6 − 5 = 1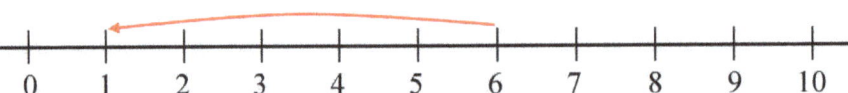

2.
a. 2 + 3 = 5	b. 4 + 6 = 10
5 − 2 = 3	10 − 4 = 6
or 5 − 3 = 2	or 10 − 6 = 4

3.

4. a. 4   b. 6   c. 9   d. 2   e. 4

Skills Review 18, p. 24

1.

a. $6 + 4 = 10$
$10 - 6 = 4$
or $10 - 4 = 6$

b. $5 + 1 = 6$
$6 - 5 = 1$
or $6 - 1 = 5$

2.
a. $3 + 2 + 3 = 8$
b. $4 + 1 + 5 = 10$
c. $4 + 3 + 2 = 9$

3. a. Three dolls have red hair. $5 + 3 = 8$ $8 - 5 = 3$
   b. There were 7 eggs left in a carton. $3 + 7 = 10$ $10 - 3 = 7$

Skills Review 19, p. 25

1. a. Numbers: 8, 2, 10.
$8 + 2 = 10$ $2 + 8 = 10$
$10 - 8 = 2$ $10 - 2 = 8$

   b. Numbers: 6, 3, 9.
$6 + 3 = 9$ $3 + 6 = 9$
$9 - 6 = 3$ $9 - 3 = 6$

2.

9	−	5	=	4
−				
6	−	2	=	4
=		−		−
3		0		1
		=		=
5	−	2	=	3

3. a. $5 + 3 + 2 = 10$ They picked a total of ten oranges.
   b. $8 - 4 = 4$ She had four pencils left.

Skills Review 20, p. 26

1. a.

   Carl: 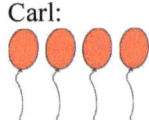   Alan: (7 balloons)

   b. Alan has seven balloons.
   c. 4 + 3 = 7

2. Please check the students' circles they drew and the answers. Answers will vary.

3. a. 5 + 2 + 3 = 10   b. 7 − 4 = 3   c. 0 + 4 = 4

Skills Review 21, p. 27

1. a. from 4 to 9 is 5 steps   b. from 3 to 7 is 4 steps   c. from 6 to 8 is 2 steps
   4 + 5 = 9   3 + 4 = 7   6 + 2 = 8

2.

3. a. There are ten turtles. There are four more turtles that are swimming.
   b. Eddie is seven years older than Dan.

Skills Review 22, p. 28

1. a. 0 + 8 + 2 = 10   b. 9 − 5 = 4   c. 4 + 4 = 8

2. a. 7 − 4 = 3
   b. 9 − 3 = 6

3. a. Megan has two fewer crayons than Alex.
   b. Cathy has seven balloons.

4. a. 3 + 6 = 9   b. 5 + 2 = 7   c. 5 + 5 = 10
      9 − 3 = 6   7 − 5 = 2   10 − 5 = 5

Chapter 3: Place Value Within 0-100

Skills Review 23, p. 29

1. a. $10 - 5 = 5$ b. $3 + 4 + 2 = 9$ c. $2 + 6 = 8$

2. a. $5 + 4 = 9$ b. $2 + 8 = 10$ c. $3 + 3 = 6$

3.

17 seventeen
13 thirteen
19 nineteen
16 sixteen
18 eighteen
14 fourteen

4. a. sixty-three, 63   b. forty-seven, 47   c. twenty-five, 25   d. seventy, 70

Skills Review 24, p. 30

1. a. $50 + 7$ b. $30 + 9$ c. $80 + 2$ d. $60 + 1$ e. $20 + 3$ f. $70 + 8$

2. a. $10 + 5 = 15$ fifteen
   b. $10 + 9 = 19$ nineteen
   c. $10 + 3 = 13$ thirteen
   d. $10 + 7 = 17$ seventeen

3. a. $8 = 8$ b. $5 > 4$ c. $3 < 5$

4. They have a total of ten books. Sarah has four more books than Matt.

Skills Review 25, p. 31

1. 15, 16, 17, 18, 19, 20, 21, 22, 23, 24, 25
   73, 74, 75, 76, 77, 78, 79, 80, 81, 82

2. The rabbit is gray = 90. The apple is green = 20. The duck is yellow = 50. The pig is pink = 60. The balloon is purple = 30. The turtle is brown = 100.

3. a. Tammy needs three more sheets of paper.
   b. Andrew saw seven cars.

Skills Review 26, p. 32

1. a. $70 + 30 = 100$ b. $80 - 20 = 60$ c. $70 - 40 = 30$
   d. $40 + 10 = 50$ e. $90 - 50 = 40$ f. $80 + 0 = 80$

2. a. $74 > 67$ b. $28 = 28$ c. $42 > 35$ d. $63 < 99$

3. a. He needs four more dollars.   b. She has four cupcakes left.

4. I am the number 63.

Skills Review 27, p. 33

1. a. 39 < 53 < 87 b. 13 < 19 < 25
   c. 37 < 56 < 60 d. 27 < 33 < 52

2. a. 116; 109   b. 123; 101   c. 140; 135

3.

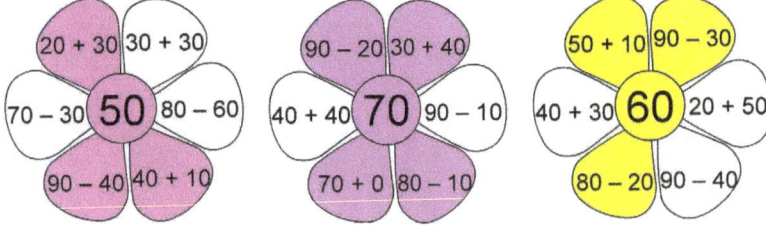

4. Sam ate two cherries.

Skills Review 28, p. 34

1.

a. 130	b. 106
hundreds / tens / ones	hundreds / tens / ones
1 3 0	1 0 6

2. a. 12, 17, 22, 27, 32, 37, 42, 47
   b. 24, 27, 30, 33, 36, 39, 42, 45

3. a. Ben has twenty sheep and fifteen rabbits.   b. Ben has more chickens than any other animal.
   c. Ben has fewer horses than any other animal.   d. Ben has two more cows than horses.

Skills Review 29, p. 35

1.	Tally Marks	Count
Apples	||||| ||||| ||	12
Pears	||||| ||||	9
Oranges	||||| ||||| ||||| |||||		21

2.

93	94	95	96	97	98	99	100	101	102
103	104	105	106	107	108	109	110	111	112
113	114	115	116	117	118	119	120	121	122

3. a. Soup   b. Chicken   c. 4

Chapter 4: Addition and Subtraction Facts

Skills Review 30, p. 36

1. a.

	Tally Marks
Balls	𝍬 𝍬 𝍬
Cars	𝍬 𝍬 𝍬 IIII
Dolls	𝍬 𝍬 𝍬 𝍬 𝍬 I
Yo-yos	𝍬 III

2. Please check the student's answer. Answers will vary.

3. a. 1   b. 5   c. 3   d. 3   e. 1   f. 2

4. Sarah is four years older than Mandy.

Skills Review 31, p. 37

1. a. Amy asked 45 people.
   b. Six more people like chocolate chip than strawberry.
   c. Thirteen people like chocolate chip.

2. a. 14, 24, 34, 44, 54, 64, 74, 84
   b. 15, 17, 19, 21, 23, 25, 27, 29

3. a. 5 + 4 = 9; 4 + 5 = 9; 3 + 6 = 9; 2 + 7 = 9; 1 + 8 = 9
   b. 80 − 20 = 60; 80 − 30 = 50; 80 − 40 = 40; 80 − 50 = 30; 80 − 60 = 20
   c. 10 + 80 = 90; 20 + 70 = 90; 30 + 60 = 90; 40 + 50 = 90; 50 + 40 = 90

4. The girls picked a total of nine flowers.

Skills Review 32, p. 38

1. a.

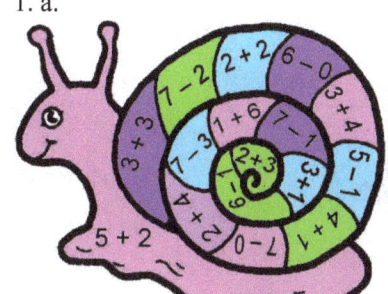

4 = blue
5 = green
6 = purple
7 = pink

2. a. 20   b. 10   c. 30   d. 30   e. 80   f. 25

3. a. Sarah and Brad have a total of 17 stickers.
   b. - c. Answers will vary. Please check the student's answers.

Skills Review 33, p. 39

1. a. $8 - 3 = 5$
   b. $2 + 4 = 6$

2.

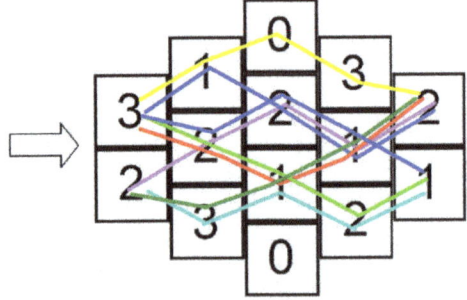

3. a. 6   b. 2   c. 5   d. 2   e. 2   f. 1

4. a. The goat pulled nine shirts off of the clothesline.
   b. Five kittens were still in the yard.

Skills Review 34, p. 40

1. Please check the student's answer. Answers will vary.

2. 1, 7, 5, 3, 4, 6, 9, 8, 0

3. a. There is a total of 28 black and blue buttons.
   b. There are four fewer blue buttons than green buttons.

4. The student doesn't need to write the combinations of numbers in this order, but the sum should always be 8.

🍎	1	2	3	4	5	6	7
🍌	7	6	5	4	3	2	1
Total	8	8	8	8	8	8	8

Skills Review 35, p. 41

1. a. Carrie collected four fewer shells than Nelson.
   b. Carrie and Eva collected fifteen shells in total.
   c. Brad and Nelson collected 23 shells in total.

2. a. 10 = 10   b. 9 < 10   c. 4 > 3   d. 2 > 1   e. 3 = 3   f. 9 < 10

3. Please check the student's answer.

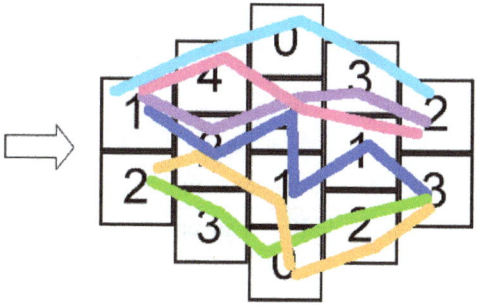

4. a. There were four roses left on the bush.
   b. Adam found ten socks.

Skills Review 36, p. 42

1.

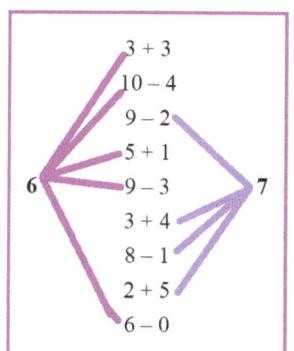

7 − 2 − 4 = green
9 − 3 − 1 = blue
10 − 2 − 2 = red
8 − 1 − 4 = yellow
5 − 0 − 1 = brown

2.

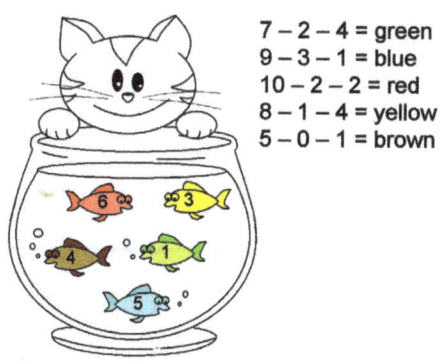

3. a. They have a total of 90 crayons.
   b. She had 30 more spoons to wash.
   c. Four puppies stayed in the box.

4. a. False   b. True   c. True   d. True   e. False   f. True

Chapter 5: Time

Skills Review 37, p. 43

1. a. 3 > 2   b. 2 < 3   c. 1 > 0

2. Please check the student's answers. Answers will vary.

3.

	a. half past two	b. nine o'clock	c. five o'clock	d. half-past six
An hour later →	half past three	ten o'clock	six o'clock	half past seven

4. The cake will be done at 3:30.

Skills Review 38, p. 44

1. a. 63   b. 67   c. 90   d. 20   e. 29   f. 70

2. a. half past nine; 9:30   b. four o'clock; 4:00   c. half past eleven; 11:30   d. one o'clock; 1:00

3. a. four hours   b. two hours   c. half an hour   d. six hours

4. a. 1   b. 3

5. Cassy has ten fewer dolls than Amanda.

6. They finished at 8:30.

Skills Review 39, p. 45

1.

5 = yellow
6 = purple
7 = red
8 = orange
9 = pink
10 = blue

2.

Now it is:	a. 8:00	b. 3:30	c. 11:00	d. 5:30	e. 1:30
1/2 hour later it is:	8:30	4:00	11:30	6:00	2:00
another 1/2 hour later:	9:00	4:30	12:00	6:30	2:30

3. a. Play a board game.   b. Draw a flower.   c. Color a picture.   d. Eat a cookie.

4. Forty ants were still carrying the cracker.

5. Four turtles were still sunning.

Skills Review 40, p. 46

1. a. 5:00   b. 10:30   c. 7:30   d. 2:00   e. 4:30

2. a. 10 = 10   b. 3 > 0   c. 2 < 4   d. 3 < 7   e. 8 = 8   f. 8 > 7

3. Please check the student's answers. Answer will vary.

4. Tomorrow, Peter will go to the dentist. Yesterday, Peter had a toothache. Today, Peter's mom calls to make an appointment.

5. The girls collected a total of one hundred leaves.

Skills Review 41, p. 47

1. a. 10   b. 3   c. 4   d. 3   e. 7   f. 2

2. August 1, August 8, August 15, August 22, August 29

3. a. open the door   b. bake a cake   c. Answers will vary.   d. watch a movie

4. a. February, March
   b. August, September
   c. November, December

5. a. Rachel baked nine pies.
   b. There are still six pies that are good enough to eat.

Chapter 6: Shapes and Measuring

Skills Review 42, p. 48

1. a. 16   b. 5

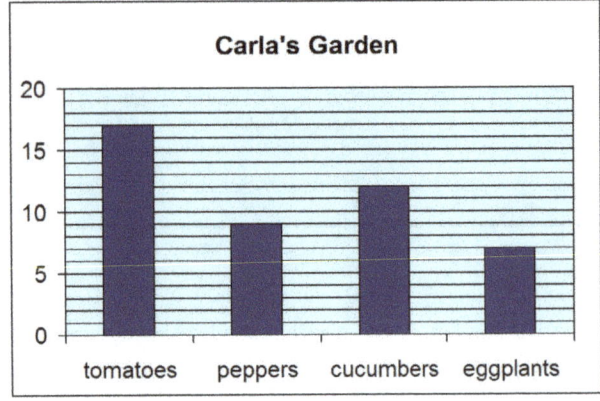

2. There are still ten butterflies on Tom's hat.

3. a. 6   b. 4   c. 4   d. 5   e. 4

4. Daddy eats lunch. PM;   It is bedtime. PM;   I get up. AM;
   Look at the fireflies! PM;   What is for breakfast? AM;   What a pretty sunset! PM

Skills Review 43, p. 49

1. May 4, May 11, May 18, May 25

2. a. take a bath   b. climb a mountain.

3. a. four sides and four corners each, they are quadrilaterals   b. three sides and three corners each, they are triangles.

4. a. He could put together a rectangle and a triangle.
   b. (1) no   (2) He made a pentagon.

Skills Review 44, p. 50

1.

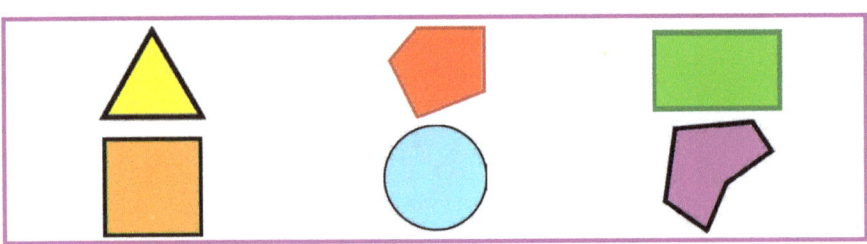

2. a. evening   b. morning   c. midday - noon

3. a. Please check the student's drawing. A triangle.

4. a. six o'clock; 6:00   b. half past ten; 10:30   c. two o'clock; 2:00   d. half past one; 1:30

Skills Review 45, p. 51

1. a. 83, 85, 87, 89, 91, 93, 95, 97
   b. 23, 27, 31, 35, 39, 43, 47, 51

2. Please check the student's work.

3.

4. a. He made 28 in total.
   b. He made more pentagons so we can assume that was his favorite shape to make.
   c. He made four more quadrilaterals than rectangles.

Skills Review 46, p. 52

1. a. Tuesday   b. October 26

2. a. 3/4   b. 1/4   c. 2/2 or 1 whole   d. 1/3

3. a. 90 = 90   b. 40 > 30   c. 50 < 70

4. a. PM   b. AM   c. PM (Assume Daddy works days.)

5. a. 51 tickets   b. 7 tickets

Skills Review 47, p. 53

1. a. =   b. >   c. <

2. Please check the student's work.

3. They have a total of 100 baseball cards.

4. They left at 10:30 A.M.

5. a. The measuring stick is longer than the xylophone. The turtle is longer than the measuring stick.
   b. The boat is longer than the measuring stick. The measuring stick is longer than the duck.

Skills Review 48, p. 54

1. a. 5 hours   b. 4 hours   c. 2 1/2 hours   d. 6 hours

2. a. 10   b. 3   c. 9   d. 5   e. 8   f. 4

3.

a. 1, 3, 2

b. 3, 2, 1

4.

5. Six monkeys are still swinging on vines.

Skills Review 49, p. 55

1. There were nine kittens.

2. a. 8:00   b. 6:30   c. 11:30   d. 1:00

3. a. 6   b. 4   c. 5

4. a. 30   b. 70   c. 100   d. 40   e. 40   f. 90

Skills Review 50, p. 56

1. The crayon is three inches long. The leaf is five inches long.

2. 53, 55, 57, 59, 61, 63, 65, 67

3. a. 4 > 3   b. 5 > 4   c. 2 > 1

4.

a. The new shapes have 3 sides, and 3 corners.
   They are triangles.

b. The new shapes have 4 sides, and 4 corners.
   They are quadrilaterals.

Skills Review 51, p. 57

1. Please check the student's answers.

2.

<u>10</u> − 8 = 2	7 − 4 = <u>3</u>	9 − 5 = <u>4</u>
3 + <u>4</u> = 7	<u>5</u> + 1 = 6	4 + <u>3</u> = 7
9 − <u>4</u> = 5	10 − 2 = <u>8</u>	2 + 8 = <u>10</u>
<u>7</u> + 2 = 9	4 + <u>5</u> = 9	9 − 7 = <u>2</u>
6 − 5 = <u>1</u>	9 − <u>2</u> = 7	5 + 1 = <u>6</u>

3. Please check the student's work.

4. a. Give the dog a bath.
   b. Bake a cake.

Chapter 7: Adding and Subtracting Within 1-100

Skills Review 52, p. 58

1. a. 5 cm b. 4 cm c. 7 cm

2. a. AM b. AM c. AM d. PM

3.
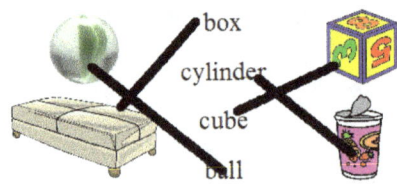

4. Vanessa needs 40 more beads to make a necklace.

5. a. 5 + 3 + 2 = 10
   b. 9 − 4 − 1 = 4

Skills Review 53, p. 59

1. Please check the student's work.

2. a. 9 < 49 < 99 b. 8 < 18 < 58 c. 10 < 70 < 100 d. 6 < 36 < 76

3. a. 9 > 8 b. 3 < 6 c. 10 = 10 d. 8 > 7

4.

a. Color two halves.	b. Color one fourth.	c. Color three quarters.	d. Color four fourths.

Skills Review 54, p. 60

1. a. 2 hours b. 1 hour c. a half hour d. four hours

2. Please check the student's work.

3. a. cube b. box

4. a. ball b. cylinder

5.

a. 14 + 2	b. 53 + 5	c. 81 + 3	d. 72 + 6
tens 1, ones 4	tens 5, ones 3	tens 8, ones 1	tens 7, ones 2
+ ↓ 2	+ ↓ 5	+ ↓ 3	+ ↓ 6
1 6	5 8	8 4	7 8

Skills Review 55, p. 61

1.
$$95 - 2 = 93$$
$$85 - 2 = 83$$
$$75 - 2 = 73$$
$$65 - 2 = 63$$
$$55 - 2 = 53$$
$$45 - 2 = 43$$
$$35 - 2 = 33$$
$$25 - 2 = 23$$

2.
   a. 5   b. 4   c. 7

3. Sharon saw twenty more butterflies than ladybugs in her garden.

4. Mike will finish practice at 11:00.

5. Today, Bill is painting his house.
   Tomorrow, Bill's house will look very different!
   Yesterday, Bill bought some paint.

6. a. $71 + 3 + 5 = 79$ b. $94 + 2 + 1 = 97$ c. $100 + 4 + 2 = 106$
      $43 + 2 + 3 = 48$ $81 + 6 + 3 = 90$ $63 + 1 + 3 = 67$

Skills Review 56, p. 62

1. Brian made 10 fewer mud pies than Carol made.

2. Please check the student's work.

3. a. 21   b. 51   c. 73   d. 31

4.

Match?		Tally Marks
yes	Hamsters	𝍸𝍷𝍷
no	Goldfish	𝍸𝍸𝍸 𝍸𝍸
no	Kittens	𝍸𝍷𝍷𝍷𝍷
yes	Puppies	𝍸𝍸𝍷𝍷
yes	Parakeets	𝍸𝍸

Skills Review 57, p. 63

1. July 7, July 14, July 21, July 28

2. Please check the student's work.
   a. False   b. False   c. True   d. True   e. True   f. True   g. False   h. True   i. True

3. a. 1 leaf, 2 pen, 3 bread
   b. 1 grasshopper, 2 baby chick, 3 kitten

4. a. 9   b. 5   c. 7   d. 3   e. 8   f. 4

Skills Review 58, p. 64

1. a. She has a total of 32 zinnias and daisies.
   b. She has 3 more daisies than petunias.
   c. Answers will vary. Please check the student's work.

2.

a. 59 + 4	b. 98 + 5	c. 47 + 6
59 + 1 + 3	98 + 2 + 3	47 + 3 + 3
60 + 3 = 63	100 + 3 = 103	50 + 3 = 53

3. Thirty minus ten equals twenty plus fifteen equals thirty-five blackbirds that love pumpkin pie!

4. He started at 4 o'clock.

5.

a.	b.	c.	d.
45 − 2 = 43	94 − 3 = 91	16 − 4 = 12	29 − 3 = 26
19 − 6 = 13	67 − 5 = 62	78 − 7 = 71	33 − 2 = 31

Skills Review 59, p. 65

1. Please check the student's answer.

2. a. ball or circle   b. cylinder   c. cube   d. box or rectangle

3. a. 56; 57   b. 81; 85   c. 46; 45   d. 64; 62

4. She had twenty strawberries left.

5. 97, 102, 107, 112, 117, 122, 127, 132

6. a. 24 < 25   b. 87 = 87   c. 49 < 50

Skills Review 60, p. 66

1. a. 5 + 5 = 10; 5 + 6 = 11   b. 9 + 1 = 10; 9 + 2 = 11   c. 7 + 3 = 10; 7 + 4 = 11

2. Peggy Pig pigged out on pumpkin pies and ate one more pie than Peter Pig ate.

3. a. 9   b. 4   c. 8   d. 7   e. 10

4. a. He needs to use an upright skinny rectangle and a short not-too-tall rectangle.
   b. Please check the student's work.

Skills Review 61, p. 67

1.

2. a. 36 + 15 = 51
   b. 19 + 19 = 38

3. a. 11   b. 17   c. 15   d. 13   e. 14   f. 14
4. a. PM   b. AM   c. PM   d. PM

Skills Review 62, p. 68

1. a. 32   b. 72   c. 43   d. 34

2.
```
40 − 40 = 0
 +
20 + 30 = 50
 =    +    −
60   50   40
      =    =
90 − 80 = 10
```

3. Please check the student's work.

4. He planted nineteen trees.

5. Seven children did not score well on the test.

Skills Review 63, p. 69

1. a. 10:30   b. 5:00   c. 12:30   d. 3:00

2. a. 86, 76, 66, 56, 46, 36, 26, 16
   b. 89, 91, 93, 95, 97, 99, 101, 103

3. a. She baked five more peanut butter cookies than chocolate chip cookies.
   b. She baked a total of 55 cookies.

4.
   a. 17 − 9
      / \
   17 − 7 − 2
      = 8

   b. 14 − 6
      / \
   14 − 4 − 2
      = 8

   c. 11 − 7
      / \
   11 − 1 − 6
      = 4

5. a. 30, 32, 40   b. 90, 95, 100   c. 100, 107, 110

Skills Review 64, p. 70

1. (1) Tim asks Mom if he can have a dog.
   (2) Mom says "yes"!
   (3) Tim takes good care of Skippy.

2. a. 106   b. 41   c. 42   d. 89

3.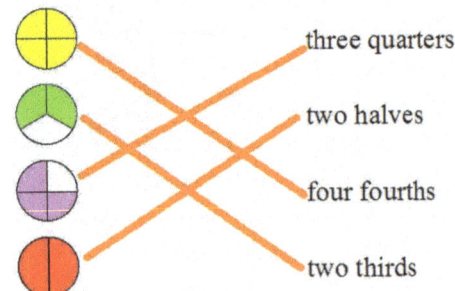

4. a. October   b. March   c. August

Chapter 8: Coins

Skills Review 65, p. 71

1. a. Gail has the fewest stuffed animals. She has six.
   b. They have a total of 20 stuffed animals.
   c. Madison has 10 more stuffed animals than Eva has.

2. a. 55¢   b. 50¢

3. a. 100   b. 90   c. 20   d. 80   e. 80   f. 30

4. a. Build a birdhouse   b. Climb a ladder.

Skills Review 66, p. 72

1. a. 12 doubles chart   b. 15 just one more than a double   c. 16 trick with nine   d. 16 doubles chart
   e. 14 trick with eight   f. 11 just one more than a double   g. 14 trick with nine   h. 11 I just know it.

2.

a. 39¢   b. 12¢

3. a. 18 < 20   b. 70 = 70   c. 45 > 44
   d. 73 = 73   e. 67 > 66   f. 34 < 37

4. a. Laura had 32 cents after she lost her cents. In the end, Laura has 52 cents.
   b. Eric finished cleaning his room at 4:30. He ate supper at 5:00.

Skills Review 67, p. 73

1. a. half past nine   b. twelve o'clock   c. half past three   d. four o'clock

2. a. She read a total of thirty pages in the book.
   b. She has twenty pages left to read.

3. a. 4 + 6 = 10; 6 + 4 = 10; 10 − 4 = 6; 10 − 6 = 4

4. a. False; 17   b. True   c. True   d. False; 14

5. a. 62¢   b. 85¢   c. 45¢

Skills Review 68, p. 74

1. a. They sold the most on Friday.
   b. They sold six more loaves on Tuesday than they sold on Thursday.
   c. They sold a total of 36 loaves of bread on Monday and Wednesday.

2. a. You pay with three quarters and three pennies. You have thirty-one cents left.
   b. You pay with one quarter, one nickel, and three pennies. You have forty-one cents left.

3. a. 99, 101, 103, 105, 107, 109, 111, 113
   b. 120, 115, 110, 105, 100, 95, 90, 85

Skills Review 69, p. 75

1. a. Fifteen people liked horses and rabbits best.
   b. Please check the student's work.

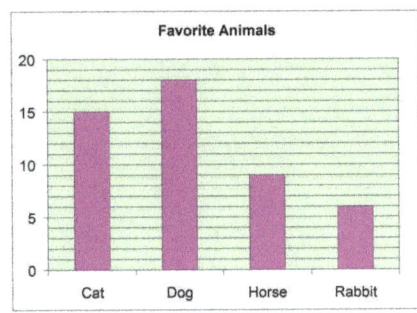

2. a. - b. Please check the student's answers.

3. She needs twenty-six cents more.

4. She can buy six stickers and will have three cents left.

Skills Review 70, p. 76

1.

a. 66 + 7	b. 85 + 6	c. 27 + 9
/ \	/ \	/ \
66 + 4 + 3	85 + 5 + 1	27 + 3 + 6
70 + 3 = 73	90 + 1 = 91	30 + 6 = 36

2. a. 9 b. 50 c. 19

3. a. The new shapes have 4 sides,
      and 4 corners.
      They are quadrilaterals.

   b. The new shapes have 3 sides,
      and 3 corners.
      They are triangles.

4. a. 60¢ b. 90¢

5. a. 94 b. 52 c. 15   30

www.ingramcontent.com/pod-product-compliance
Lightning Source LLC
Chambersburg PA
CBHW081026040426
42444CB00014B/3362